# It's a Dog's Life

Written by Kerri Lane
Illustrated by Ned Culic

Published by Pearson Education Limited, 80 Strand, London, WC2R 0RL.

www.pearsonschools.co.uk

First published in 2010 by Pearson Australia.
This edition of *It's a Dog's Life* is published by Pearson Education Limited by arrangement with Pearson Australia. All rights reserved.

Text © Pearson Australia 2010
Text by Kerri Lane

Original illustrations © Pearson Australia 2010
Illustrated by Ned Culic

22 21 20 19 18
10 9 8 7 6 5 4 3 2 1

**British Library Cataloguing in Publication Data**
A catalogue record for this book is available from the British Library

ISBN 978 0 435 19455 0

**Copyright notice**
All rights reserved. No part of this publication may be reproduced in any form or by any means (including photocopying or storing it in any medium by electronic means and whether or not transiently or incidentally to some other use of this publication) without the written permission of the copyright owner, except in accordance with the provisions of the Copyright, Designs and Patents Act 1988 or under the terms of a licence issued by the Copyright Licensing Agency, Barnards Inn, 86 Fetter Lane, London EC4A 1EN (www.cla.co.uk). Applications for the copyright owner's written permission should be addressed to the publisher.

Printed in China by Golden Cup

**Acknowledgements**
We would like to thank the following schools for their invaluable help in the development and trialling of the Bug Club resources: Bishop Road Primary School, Bristol; Blackhorse Primary School, Bristol; Hollingwood Primary School, West Yorkshire; Kingswood Parks Primary, Hull; Langdale CE Primary School, Ambleside; Pickering Infant School, Pickering; The Royal School, Wolverhampton; St Thomas More's Catholic Primary School, Hampshire; West Park Primary School, Wolverhampton.

**Note from the publisher**
Pearson has robust editorial processes, including answer and fact checks, to ensure the accuracy of the content in this publication, and every effort is made to ensure this publication is free of errors. We are, however, only human, and occasionally errors do occur. Pearson is not liable for any misunderstandings that arise as a result of errors in this publication, but it is our priority to ensure that the content is accurate. If you spot an error, please do contact us at resourcescorrections@pearson.com so we can make sure it is corrected.

# Contents

**Chapter 1**
Grandma! Where Are Your Manners?  5

**Chapter 2**
What's Going On?  10

**Chapter 3**
A Family of Dogs  15

**Chapter 4**
Good Joke!  19

**Chapter 5**
Grandma's Cheese Biscuits  25

**Chapter 6**
Mr Wishbone to the Rescue  30

**Chapter 7**
The Pepper Swap  37

**Chapter 8**
Anyone for Salt?  42

## Chapter 1

# Grandma! Where Are Your Manners?

The fifth of September was probably the weirdest day of my whole life. I knew at once that I would never, ever forget that day. For a start, I had been to the dentist and got my new braces fitted, but that wasn't the reason I would always remember it…

It all began at dinner. Everyone else had Grandma's Special Chicken. I didn't. I had tomato soup out of a tin. I love tomato soup out of a tin – it's a lot better than the stuff Mum makes. It was a special treat because my mouth was sore.

The whole family was sitting around the table when the first weird thing happened.

Grandma scratched her ear. It wasn't the scratching that worried me. It was the *way* she scratched her ear that was odd. She did it with her foot!

Now can you see why I was puzzled?

"Grandma!" I whispered.

## Grandma! Where Are Your Manners?

I like Grandma, and I didn't want her to get into trouble with Mum. Mum has very strict rules about table manners. I didn't think scratching your ear with your foot was the kind of thing she would approve of.

Grandma just went on scratching. "Nothing like a good scratch, I always say," she said.

When had she said that? I'd *never* heard her say that!

I looked at Mum – I was sure she would look as though she was going to explode, but Mum didn't even seem to notice Grandma's scratching. That's because she had her head in her plate! Right in her plate – she was licking it clean!

"Mum?"

Mum looked up at me. Her eyes were bright and a big **blob** of chicken gravy dripped off her nose. There was even some on her eyebrow. "Yes, Gus?" she replied calmly.

Gus? What was going on? Mum never called me Gus. She always made everybody call me by my real name, "Angus".

Mum was still looking at me. I was about to ask her what was happening when she looked at my bowl.

"You've left a little bit of soup," she said, licking her lips. "Do you want it?"

I looked down and frowned. The only thing in my bowl was a tiny scraping of tomato soup, stuck to the side. "I guess not…" I said

"Good," said Mum, reaching for my bowl.

As I watched what happened next, I couldn't believe my eyes. Somehow I knew I'd never be able to tell my friends Ethan and Bryce. I'd try, but they'd never believe me.

**Chapter 2**

# What's Going On?

You see, Mum leaned over my bowl and flicked out her tongue. Then she licked the whole bowl until it shone!

She licked my bowl! "Mmmm," she murmured.

## What's Going On?

Suddenly the light bulb in my brain flicked on. Of course! This was a joke! And everyone knew about it except me. I swallowed a grin. It was better than most of the jokes my family come up with. Most of their jokes are pretty lame. This one was a bit weird, but actually quite funny. They were probably waiting to see if I would crack, and then they'd all laugh and say "Gotcha!" Then they'd tease me about it for ages.

Well, this time I wouldn't give in. I'd keep a straight face if it killed me. And it probably would – Mum had looked so funny! I couldn't even look at my sister, Nikki, because I'd crack up with laughter. So I just closed my eyes and waited.

When nothing else happened, I opened one eye and peeked at Dad. At least he looked normal. He was standing up, with his plate in his hands. It looked pretty clean, too, except for the chicken bones.

"I'll be back in a minute," he said. "I'm just going to bury these bones in the back garden."

"Bury these bones"? They were really determined to make me crack. This was one of their best jokes ever! I nodded to him, trying so hard not to laugh. "That's a good one, Dad."

Dad smiled. "Would you like a game of fetch after dinner, Gus?"

"Fetch?" I asked, half choking as I said it. "People don't play fetch, Dad, dogs play fet– "

I didn't get to finish my sentence, because suddenly all eyes were on Grandpa.

Nikki's cat had wandered past the door. Grandpa jumped out of his chair and took off after it!

Out of the back door they went. Grandpa chased that cat right up the tree in our back garden.

## What's Going On?

Well, Grandpa didn't run up the tree, only the cat. Grandpa just leaned his paws – I mean, hands – against the trunk and made funny barking noises.

At the same time, our dog Charlie came bounding straight in through the back door. He dived right under the table and plonked both paws over his eyes. I didn't blame him.

I looked over at Nikki. She was licking her hands, just like Charlie licks his paws after he's rolled in his food. At least she hadn't rolled in her food. Had she?

"I know what you're all doing, Nik. You can stop fooling around now," I whispered.

Nikki looked up. "What are you talking about? Want a drink?" Then she stuck her tongue in the glass of water in front of her.

"Not like that, I don't!" I yelped. Nikki was slurping like a dog and water was going everywhere!

## Chapter 3

# A Family of Dogs

Grandpa walked back into the kitchen. I must have been staring at Nikki, because he stopped and frowned. "What's the matter with you, young Gus?"

I was about to answer when he looked through the doorway into the living room. Then his face lit up. "The sofa's free! The sofa's free! It's mine! It's mine!"

I followed him and watched him leap onto the sofa, and let out a loud, contented sigh.

This was getting too silly.

"It's no big deal, Grandpa – it's only the sofa!" I said.

"Shh!" he ordered. "They'll make me lie on the floor if they catch me!"

Then he rolled onto his back with both arms and legs in the air.

I was getting sick of this game. "Maybe I'll just go to bed," I said.

Mum was still in the kitchen, scratching her belly.

"You know, Mum, this isn't April Fools' Day," I said. "It's September!"

"That's nice." She didn't even look at me as she spoke. Instead, her eyes were rolling in circles as she watched a fly that was busily buzzing around her.

I wondered what she would do if she caught the fly. Perhaps she was planning to eat it? Suddenly I started to feel a little bit sick. If only Mum would turn back into her normal self!

As I was leaving the room, I spotted Dad coming in through the back door. He had Charlie's lead in his mouth. "Walkies!" he called in a sing-song voice. "Who wants to go walkies?"

This was too much! I was living with a family of dogs!

## Chapter 4

# Good Joke!

The next day was Saturday, thank goodness. I wasn't sure what to expect when I walked into the kitchen. Everything looked normal – at least so far. I'd spent all night thinking about what had happened to my family, and I thought I had the answer.

This was my theory: some kind of dog aliens had taken over my family. Maybe it was an experiment. Perhaps they were planning to take over Earth and my family just happened to be the guinea pigs! They would probably need to have dog spies or dog agents already living in our house. I looked over at Charlie who was snoring loudly in the corner. Then again, maybe not.

Charlie was certainly no Super Spy Dog, which meant I had to try to find another reason for my family behaving like dogs.

There was no time to lose! I also needed to work out why I hadn't been affected. I hadn't worked that bit out yet.

All I knew was that I had to look after my family – at least until I could solve this problem and get them back to normal. After all, "doggie people" or not, they were still *my* people. I was all they had.

Dad was on his way outside when I reached the table.

"Going for nice walkies? Do you want me to get the lead for you?" I asked.

Dad stopped and stared at me. "What a strange question. Are you all right?"

Mum was finishing her breakfast. She smiled up at me. "Good morning, Angus. Did you have a good sleep?"

"Not really," I mumbled.

"Perhaps a nice bowl of muesli will make you feel better. Would you put my bowl in the sink while I get some juice?"

Cereal was stuck to the sides of the bowl and there was some milk in the bottom. "Don't you want to lick it clean?" I asked.

Mum frowned. "What on earth are you talking about? It's very bad manners to lick a plate! You should know that, Angus."

Just then, Grandma walked in. I started rubbing her back. "Nothing like a good scratch, isn't that right, Grandma?" Grandma pulled away. She looked at Mum. "What's the matter with Angus? He's acting very strangely."

"I know, but he isn't the only one." Mum was staring at Charlie, the *real* dog.

Charlie was lying on the floor with his paws over his eyes again. He lifted one and stared at us for a moment, then gave a huge yawn and went to sleep.

# A Family of Dogs

"I don't know what's the matter with this dog," said Mum. "I gave him some doggie vitamins, but they don't seem to be working. He won't even eat his breakfast."

What was happening? Was my family normal again? Suddenly, I burst out laughing. "I get it now! You really *were* playing a trick on me last night, weren't you?"

"What are you talking about, Angus?" asked Mum.

"When you were pretending to be dogs! Oh boy, you really had me fooled!"

They all looked at me, then at each other.

"We've no idea what you're talking about, Angus," Dad said. "We weren't playing tricks on you last night."

"Yeah, right!" Just then, a car horn honked loudly. "That'll be Ethan. His mum's taking us swimming this morning, remember? I've got to go."

At the door I turned back and laughed again. "You really had me with that joke!"

## Chapter 5
# Grandma's Cheese Biscuits

Ethan, Bryce and I had races up and down the pool and took it in turns to see who could do the best dives. It was a long morning, and we were all starving when we got back to my house.

Bryce sniffed the air. "Mmmm, it smells like your grandma has been baking again."

"Yes," I said. "Smells like Grandma's cheese biscuits. You'll love them."

We raced into the kitchen and dived into the plate of biscuits Grandma had set out on the table.

The rest of the family was already seated, and everyone shuffled around to make room for us.

Just as I thought, Bryce and Ethan did love the biscuits. I would have, too, if I'd been able to eat any. Unfortunately, I didn't even get to taste one tiny piece! As soon as I stretched open my mouth, it started to hurt again. The dentist had said it would take a few days to get used to these new braces. It looked like it was tomato soup again for me.

It took me a few minutes to find some and heat it up on the cooker.

When I turned around again, everyone had gone crazy. This time it wasn't just my family who were acting like dogs – it was Ethan and Bryce too!

Oh no! It was starting all over again.

Bryce was standing on the chair and stretching across the table. Ethan and Nikki were both chewing on the table legs. Grandma had her face in her plate, Dad was chasing flies and Mum was scratching.

Grandpa was the worst. He'd shoved his face right under the kitchen tap so it was all wet, and now he was shaking his head from side to side. He reminded me of Charlie when he's just had a bath. Drops of water flew everywhere!

This was getting serious. What had made them change? My head was spinning. I tried to think. All they had done was eat Grandma's cheese biscuits.

That light bulb flashed on inside my head again. *Grandma's biscuits!* Suddenly, I knew what was making my family act like dogs.

Well, I sort of knew … my head was buzzing. They were all eating something they shouldn't eat. But what? Cheese biscuits and Grandma's Special Chicken? That didn't make sense. So what was happening?

## Chapter 6

# Mr Wishbone to the Rescue

I gulped down the soup and tried to ignore everyone while I thought about what to do. Only one person could help me – Mr Wishbone down at the Crazy Cow Pet Shop.

Leaving the rest of them to their doggie deeds, I jumped on my bike and raced to his shop. I hoped it would still be open.

## Mr Wishbone to the Rescue

Mr Wishbone was a thin man, with a huge beaky nose just like a parrot. He frowned as he listened to my story.

"Hmm. You certainly have a problem," he agreed. "I've only ever heard of one other case like this, but that was quite different. That time, it was when some dog aliens tried to take over Earth."

My eyes nearly popped out of my head. "Really?"

"No, I made it up. It sounds really good though, doesn't it?" Mr Wishbone didn't laugh like other people. Instead, his eyes sparkled and his beaky nose twitched.

It was twitching now.

I couldn't believe I nearly fell for that! "Oh. Right. Hilarious," I mumbled. "So, what can I do about *my* problem?"

"Yes, I'm sorry. We must be serious. Well, first we have to discover what they've eaten. I'll tell you what, just let me lock up and I'll come home with you," said Mr Wishbone. "Is that a spare helmet on the back of your bike?"

As soon as we got inside my house, Mr Wishbone's nose started twitching very fast. Nikki was still chewing on the table leg, but everyone else was asleep on the floor. All of them were snoring. Very loudly.

The newspaper was torn to shreds and Grandma's slippers were chewed at the toes. Yuck! Those slippers ponged. I certainly didn't fancy making a meal of them, but someone had!

Mr Wishbone looked at the table. "Mmmm, cheese biscuits! They're my favourite! Do you mind if I–"

I grabbed his hand. "No!" I yelled over all the snoring.

Mr Wishbone looked hurt. "Oh, I see. I didn't mean to be rude. You seemed to have plenty."

"No, you don't understand. That's what the others ate before they started acting like dogs."

He frowned. "It's not dog food. I thought they may have eaten dog food."

"We don't eat dog food!"

"Oh, of course not!" Mr Wishbone shook his head. "But dog food is the only thing I can think of that might cause this."

Just then, Charlie wandered up and flopped at my feet.

Mr Wishbone frowned again as he looked at Charlie.

"Goodness me, Charlie. What you need is a good dose of dog vitamins."

I sniffed the biscuits for clues. "Yes, but Mum bought him some, and they didn't work."

Mr Wishbone scratched his head.

"I remember that now. Your mum bought those special dog vitamins, the ones that really pep up your dog."

Charlie was looking at the biscuits. He still hadn't eaten his breakfast. Suddenly, I had an idea. "I wonder what would happen if–"

"Wait!" Mr Wishbone grabbed my hand just as I was about to feed Charlie a biscuit. "What if he starts acting like a human? He'll start bossing you around."

Mr Wishbone paused for a moment, then continued in a rush. "Goodness, he might even take over my pet shop! After all, he'd be able to talk to the animals better than I could!"

I shook my head. "I don't think so. As a matter of fact, I've just had an idea. What do these vitamins look like?"

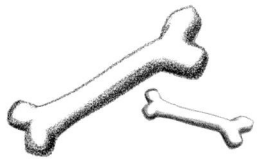

"Well, it's a powder. A fine red powder. You sprinkle it on the dog's food. It's called Peppy Pet Powder."

## Chapter 7
# The Pepper Swap

I went to the pantry and took out a plastic container marked "Charlie's Vitamins".

"Grandma always takes everything out of its packet and puts it into a container," I explained. "As soon as the shopping arrives home, she starts unpacking and re-packing. Nothing is still in its original wrapping."

I handed the container to Mr Wishbone. "Are these the vitamins?"

Mr Wishbone poked his finger in the container. Then he held his finger to his nose. Suddenly, that long beaky nose was twitching like it had never twitched before. But this time, he wasn't laughing.

Instead, the biggest sneeze I've ever heard echoed around the room.

"Oh dear …" He sniffed, but I could see another explosion building up so I got him some tissues.

I frowned as I tried to work out what he'd discovered. "What's the matter? Are the vitamins bad?"

"No." He sniffed again. "It's pepper! Very hot, red pepper!"

"Pepper?" I stopped dead still. Of course!

Racing back to the pantry I grabbed the container marked "Red Pepper".

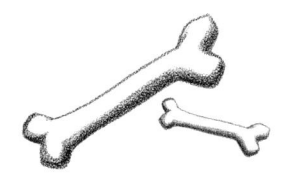

## The Pepper Swap

Mr Wishbone backed away when I gave him the new container.

"Just smell it," I said. "Please?"

"Oh, all right." Holding his tissue close to his nose, Mr Wishbone poked one finger into the red powder and gently sniffed.

I waited, but this time there was no sneeze. "It's not pepper, is it?"

Mr Wishbone raised his eyebrows. "No, it's not. In fact, it smells like–"

"Dog vitamins?"

Mr Wishbone nodded. "Someone must have mixed them up. Does your grandma use red pepper in the biscuits *and* her special chicken?"

I nodded. "Yes. She once told me it was her secret ingredient. No wonder Charlie wouldn't eat his food! It was sprinkled with red pepper! Grandma swapped the pepper with the vitamins!"

Smiling, I looked back at my family and friends, who were now all sleeping.

This would wear off soon, just like it had last time, and they wouldn't remember any of it. I knew they probably wouldn't believe me, so I decided not to tell them. I'd clean up the mess and change the labels on the containers. Then I'd just wait for them to wake up, and everyone would be normal again.

## Chapter 8

# Anyone for Salt?

Two weeks had passed since that day, and so far everyone was still normal. Not a bark or lick from any of them. Hurrying up the steps from cricket training, my tummy rumbled and I wondered what we'd be having for dinner.

Dinner. Every time I heard the word I remembered that night when the family started acting like dogs. I'd still never told any of them what had happened.

Grandma and Mum would freak out if they knew what they'd been doing. Scratching and licking bowls! What a sight!

I grinned as I raced through the door. Everyone was already sitting at the kitchen table eating.

"Good, you're home, Angus," said Dad. "Wash your hands and sit down. I'll give you some of Grandma's Special Chicken."

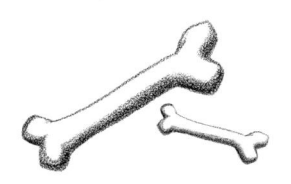

I stifled another huge grin. "Grandma's Special Chicken, eh?"

I struggled not to laugh as the memories of last time came flooding back. Hopefully this meal would be different. It smelled great.

I reached for the salt. Then my smile froze. In fact, all of me froze. I couldn't move a muscle as my eyes glued themselves to the centre of the table.

There, instead of the salt shaker, was a container with white stuff in it. It looked like salt, but on the label it read "Nikki's Cat's Vitamins". It was in Grandma's handwriting.

245

Suddenly, my head was spinning again. My eyes unglued themselves and darted around the table so fast I could hardly take in what I was seeing.

*No!* Barely able to breathe, I took in the scene more slowly. My eyes weren't deceiving me. I *had* seen it!

Every single member of my family had a bowl of milk sitting in front of them. Mum was licking her arms clean. Grandpa was stroking his ears. The rest had their heads down and were drinking straight from their bowls.

I grabbed my head with both hands. *Oh no! Not again!*

Then all their heads came up at once and everyone yelled, "Gotcha!" They were all pointing at me, laughing and patting each other on the back.

I sank into the chair. "You were joking!" Then it dawned on me. "Ah! You found out about the mix-up with Charlie's vitamins, didn't you?"

Grandpa nodded, still choking back his laughter. "Yes, Mr Wishbone told me all about it today when I got these vitamins for the cat. What a sight we must have been! I can hardly believe it!"

I laughed. *Whew!* What a relief. "I thought you really believed you were cats. I'm so glad that it was just a joke!"

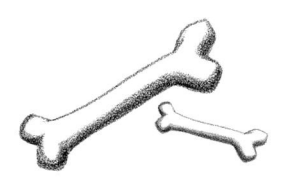

Then Nikki meowed. Nobody but me seemed to notice. My heart started to race. At least, I hoped it was a joke…